Contents

Introduction

The Advancing Guitarist faces many challenges on the instrument, yet it is one of the most exciting periods in a player's development. This book features hacks, mini-lessons, insights, tricks and tips to push you past your new-found comfort zone and make real progress on the instrument. You will reach many plateaus as you progress on guitar, and these are fantastic opportunities to do something different, and to learn something new while deepening the knowledge you've already acquired. This book provides solutions to many of the issues faced by guitarists on the intermediate plateau, those stuck in a rut, or those simply wishing to break into advanced territory on the instrument. I hope to be a facilitator on this journey, and help you get to where you want to be with your guitar playing.

To your best playing yet,

Graham

www.unlocktheguitar.net

1. The Secret to Fast Playing that Everyone Overlooks

I was never obsessed with playing fast, but I thought it would be interesting to learn the techniques and the ins and outs of picking and pick control. It seems that everyone gets hold of these tapes (DVDs nowadays) of players like Yngwie Malmsteen, Paul Gilbert, Michael Angelo Batio and so on, and attempt the monster runs they see their heroes knock out like picking machines. This is all well and good, but wouldn't it be more useful to learn the techniques or practice runs they used to do to get to that point? To be able to copy those licks, you need to have already developed your own speed techniques. The (slightly ironic) problem is that most guitarists are watching these tapes in the hopes of acquiring those very techniques—something that's rarely explained.

In the case of Michael Angelo Batio, I was watching an interview where he demonstrated a run he used to do when developing his speed technique. I was surprised to see that it contained very few notes and was just basically crossing to the adjacent string at high speed. If you think about it, copying a monster lick that crosses the whole fretboard, or running up and down three-octave scale patterns, involves way too many factors such as pick control, changing strings, pick direction etc. that are far easier to get under control by restricting your speed practice to a sequence that just involves the fundamentals of speed playing on two adjacent strings: accurate picking and the ability to change strings easily. These movements can then be expanded to other strings when you've built up speed and control on two strings. In this way you're almost 'retracing the steps' of speed players in order to construct your own fast playing technique.

What to do: Find a repeatable sequence of notes on two adjacent strings that involves either alternate or economy picking as well as string changing and practice it to death. When you have it under control, and can play it fairly fast and comfortably, expand it across the fretboard and into those monster patterns.

2. How to Move Beyond Pentatonic Scales

Most guitarists reach this wall at some point: they're stuck in minor pentatonic/blues scale based playing, and are bored to tears of it. You may think the next thing to do would be to learn some theory, or venture into the dreaded modes, but wait! Pentatonic scales are used in all kinds of music, even jazz! If you only play and listen to four-on-the-floor rock, then you have no references outside of that i.e. you don't even know what not playing pentatonic scales is supposed to sound like, so where are you going to get your inspiration/ideas from? The man that helped me get through this stage and out the other side was John Scofield. Here's a player with rock roots who can play any kind of jazz or fusion guitar styles at the drop of a hat. It's even better if you go chronologically through his career as you can see the progression. The Uberjam albums are especially good listening as you'll hear a fusion of rock, funk, and jazz—and plenty of pentatonic playing.

What I'm saying here is that as you develop as a guitar player, you'll find you're very much a product of your influences, and these influences are your reference for phrasing, dynamics, note choice and much more besides. Therefore, if you can draw inspiration from players who are not, in this case, rock-pentatonic oriented, your ear is going to latch on to new phrasing ideas and create a reference for your own improvisation, which will then lead you to come up with more advanced phrasing ideas, and give you the impetus to study the theory behind it.

3. Do You Need a Mentor Rather than a Teacher?

All things considered, if you're an advancing guitarist, the role of the guitar teacher in 2016 is almost redundant due to the advent of the internet. There are, of course, plenty of guitar teachers that are still teaching as if it were the mid-90s, and this is great if you rely on, or are motivated by that one-on-one attention.

If I were to have lessons again now, I would seek out a mentor as oppose to a guitar teacher. A mentor is a guide who can help the mentee find the right direction and develop solutions to playing issues. Mentors rely upon having had similar experiences to gain an empathy with the mentee and an understanding of their issues. Mentoring provides the mentee with an opportunity to think about their playing and progress. For me it would be someone whose playing I admire, and who I think would be able to provide me with the insight I won't find on the internet. They don't have to be a teacher per se, just someone who's an accomplished player, and who's willing to take the time to provide me with the insight I need to achieve my playing goals. The mentor-apprentice relationship is something that the internet can't do, other than provide the means of communication, and with the right person it can be truly inspiring.

4. How to Get into Melodic Soloing

The advancing guitarist usually has a good amount of technique, which at this point is a double-edged sword because the tendency is to go for more speed, more technique and more flash. What you should really be doing is slowing things down and becoming more melodic; you may even feel like something is missing from your improvisations—and this is usually strong melodic content. There are plenty of ways you could do this such as focusing on triads, coming up with melodies in your head and then trying to play them on the guitar, and so on. While these things are very useful, they all lack a certain dynamic which only occurs when the solo has a wider purpose, which is why I highly recommend sitting down and writing (not improvising) guitar solos for actual songs. It's only by doing this that you bring in factors such as: what the song's about, what fits the song, the right tone for the song, etc. You'll be surprised at what you're capable of when these elements come into play. The best material to use for this is own songs, or failing that someone else's. You can also find songs without solos and set yourself the task of writing the solo for that particular song. Once you've done this a few times, you'll start to see more melodic ideas creeping into your improvised solos.

5. How to Use the Other Four Minor Pentatonic Boxes

Guitarists tend to get fixated on box 1 of the minor pentatonic scale and milk it to death. You may know the shapes for the other four boxes, but how often do you actually use them? Box 1 is by far the most usable and instantly gratifying of the minor pentatonic boxes, so much so that it creates this phobia of using the others. This can be solved in the following way:

In Box 1 it's very easy to 'get hold' of the sound and pretty much play what you want to hear after a while. This is not so easy with the other four boxes, but what you can do is practice in the following way by simply transferring the sounds you know so well from Box 1 to the other Boxes.

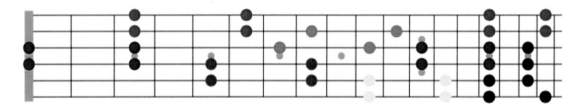

In the above diagram you can see G Minor Pentatonic Box 1 up at the 15th fret. The (Layla) notes in red are then marked in other colors down the fretboard. They are the exact same notes, but now you can see how they repeat through the other pentatonic boxes. It figures that whatever you can play up at the 15th fret, you can play at any other location where the same notes are available, including the bends, licks and melodies you would do. Note that the green notes are still the same pattern, they're just offset by the fretboard—the distance from the G string to the B string is a major third, not a fourth like all the other strings.

Check out the next set of notes:

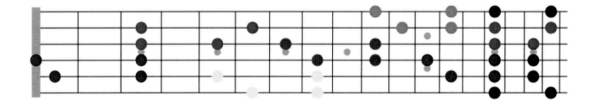

This time we have a four-note pattern in red in box 1 up at the 15th fret that's already offset by the fretboard as mentioned above. This is why all the other patterns are different but consistent. These are the same notes you play in Box 1, just in different places, and boxes, on the rest of the neck. Hopefully by drawing your attention to this fact, you'll start to feel confident about using the other four boxes.

Now that you've gotten the hang of this, see if you can work out remaining sets of patterns, and how they repeat, for yourself.

6. Why Your Solos Still Sound like Scales and How to Turn It Around

If your soloing sounds like scales or arpeggios it means that the scale/arpeggio is still dictating what you play most of the time. You may have moments of 'inspiration' when you manage to exert what you want to play, but most of the time the scale dictates. Try to redress the balance by dictating to the guitar what you want to play, not the other way around. It's a tough thing to do because as guitar players we spend so long playing shapes and patterns, and not nearly the same amount of time coming up with phrasing and melodies. If you think about this, it's probably the same ratio as scalar type stuff to moments of inspiration in your solos. You can turn this ratio around by first of all slowing down, as speed will all but eradicate your ability to think about what you're playing, and then asking yourself if you really wanted to play what you just played or whether the scale dictated it to you. Playing up and down one string, or two adjacent strings is also a great way to start dictating what you want to play as there are no patterns, and it's easier hit the note you want when you see horizontal distances as oppose to vertical ones.

7. What's Your Specialty?

Learning guitar is similar in structure to studying medicine. You study general guitar for about 7 or so years, you do plenty of live practice (hopefully without killing anyone), and then you study a specialty or two. My point is that most of us mere mortals cannot master everything in one lifetime, so it's probably worth pursuing one or two styles that you're drawn to, or that you've become really good at playing after about 7 or 8 years of trying to master everything. At this point it's worth asking for someone else's opinion on what you're good at because you'll find it difficult to be objective. People would always remark on my blues playing, but I'd play it down a lot as I never found it a particularly hard style to learn. I would be drawn to mastering more complex things that I actually struggled with, instead of noticing what was staring me in the face. Your specialty (or specialties) are the styles that come naturally to you. These can actually be hard to identify because we tend to dismiss them due to the lack of challenge, believing that we must conquer some hard-to-do thing to arrive at God-like guitar status. So ask a friend or two, and you'll begin to see what style(s) people associate you with as a player, then pursue it.

8. When to Learn the Notes on the Neck

If you haven't learned the notes on the neck yet, don't feel too bad about it; perhaps it wasn't the right time. If the internet is making you feel guilty for not learning them, or convincing you there's a secret method to learn them in X number of minutes, hours or days, then don't believe that either. Learning the notes on the neck is incredibly useful, but is also part of a bigger picture and works in conjunction with other elements in music; in isolation it has no real power. You just don't see internet sites saying, 'Learn the notes on the piano and become a piano master!' Or something to that effect. Why not? Well, try it out. You can learn the notes on a piano in all of 5 minutes or so... Did you become a piano master? If you could do the same on guitar, you wouldn't become a guitar master either; it's just easier to sell the idea because it takes time, and when you've learned all the notes on the neck it's too late to get your money back.

Anyway, all this goes to show that learning the notes on the neck facilitates other things such as music theory or sight-reading, or understanding the shapes you're playing on a deeper level. If you're interested in any of those things, or are currently studying them, then it's time to learn the notes on the neck. If not, you can leave it on the back-burner.

9. How to Get the Gig

If you don't sing already, I'd highly recommend learning to do so as it's an incredibly useful skill for any advancing guitarist. Not only does it make you more versatile within a band, it also increases your chances of getting hired at an audition. If they're looking for someone who can play and sing a little, or do backing vocals, you're going to get the gig over all the guys or gals that may be able to play rings around you, but can't sing.

There are then three elements that are critical to the success of any audition:

1. Preparation

It goes without saying that you can never be over-prepared. If you've been given material to learn you need to learn it and then some. Preparation also involves researching the artist or band you're hoping to join, both on a musical and personal level, so you can get a better idea of what they like and don't like. You must listen extensively to the artist's back catalog as this will give you a feel for the artist's music. Any decent musician can replicate an artist's work on a technical level but few can bring the right feel into the equation, and these are the guys and girls that get hired. Remember the

6 Ps: Proper Preparation Prevents Piss-Poor Performance; over-prepare but don't overplay, most of the time whoever's doing the hiring wants to see what you can bring to the situation rather than how good (you think) you are. Leave your ego at the door.

2. Attitude

Attitude is almost everything but what's the right attitude to have? It's a difficult thing to describe but I think Mike Mangini's attitude during the Dream Theater drummer auditions a few years ago (check out the documentary that was made) really encapsulates the perfect attitude to have if you want to get the gig. Mike is literally brimming with positivity and enthusiasm, there is no doubt in his mind that he's the next Dream Theater drummer; his preparation is flawless and the vibe he transmits is reciprocated by the band members.

3. Image

The third piece of the jigsaw is (unfortunately) image. We were told this on the very first day of Music College, and it was drilled into us throughout the course, although most of the guitarists scoffed at the idea of doing any kind of personal grooming. Truth be told if you want to make a career out of music then you need to look after and tailor your image to the gigs you're going for. If you happen to be one of those people who can shape-shift chameleon-like into any genre, then use this to your advantage. If you're strictly [insert name of genre] then stick to that genre as you'll be wasting your time if you're unwilling to work on your look. Getting your head around the dynamic of the gig should also be part of your preparation; think of yourself as the solution to the hiring artist or band's problem by understanding **what they require from you**.

10. How to Learn New Scales without Learning New Patterns

You may have noticed that you don't really use the major scale explicitly when playing. It is the mother of all scales, but more so in a theoretical sense because it has a neutral set of intervals: 1, 2, 3, 4, 5, 6, 7; i.e. there are no sharp/flat intervals to contend with.

I'm assuming that by now you have a relatively good grasp of the modes and how to apply them to your playing. I'm also assuming that you're well-versed with intervals. If you're able to identify the intervals you're playing as you play them, you will also be able to incorporate new scales into your playing by replacing intervals rather than learning a bunch of new patterns. This is particularly useful when building on the modes you already know. Simply identify the interval and replace it to get a different mode. You may recognize some of these 'new' scales as the modes of the melodic and harmonic minor scales, which they are; this is just another way of seeing them on the fretboard.

Original Mode	Interval to Replace	Resulting Mode
Ionian	6 with b6	Ionian b6 or Harmonic Major
Dorian	4 with #4	Dorian #4
	2 with b2	Dorian b2
Phrygian	b3 with 3	Phrygian Dominant
Lydian	2 with #2	Lydian #2
	7 with b7	Lydian Dominant
	5 with #5	Lydian Augmented
Mixolydian	6 with b6	Mixolydian b6 or Hindu
	2 with b2	Mixolydian b2
Aeolian	5 with b5	Aeolian b5 of Half-diminished
Locrian	4 with b4	Altered Scale

11. How to Balance Your Pickups for a Sharper Sound

This is one of the guitar tech's secret weapons for making any guitar's clarity from string to string sound crystal-clear while improving the overall tone of the guitar.

1. Plug your guitar into anything with a level meter such as an 8-track, or one of any number of apps or programs that have this feature; some tuners even have them.

2. Play each string individually while adjusting the pickup height so that the output of each string is at the same level according to the level meter.

3. Do this for each pickup on your guitar until they're all at the same level.

You'll probably find that the pickups need lowering at the bass end, and that there's a marked difference in the overall string-to-string clarity, even on a cheap guitar.

12. Write This Down Before Every Practice Session

Do yourself and your guitar playing an immense favor by writing out and completing this statement before every practice session:

'By the end of this practice session, I will be able to _____ **'**

Keep it where you can see it so that you don't get distracted. You're doing this because a practice session without a goal is virtually pointless. If your practice session does not have a final objective (be sure to choose something you can accomplish within your practice time), it will become unproductive and deteriorate into mindless noodling, playing everything you know, and then going on to your next activity.

Try to make your practice sessions as real as possible; this means they should reflect what you do when you're actually playing live. Play through your amp with your usual set-up, and don't use headphones because they completely change the sound, and you start getting used to a sound that you're never going to use live. Stand up when you practice too; you can't groove sitting down! Plus, a lot of the time when you master something sitting down, you go to play it standing up and it's a whole different kettle of fish.

13. How to Get Free Gear

Okay, that was more of a catchy title but let me tell you what will eventually lead you to getting tons of free gear without even asking for it.

I imagine that if you're reading this, you've gotten good at guitar and you might be wondering if you can take it to the next level and actually make a living from it. Of course you can, and I really hope you do!

Now, all that money you're about to spend on expensive gear, because you've gotten a little bit good, spend it on promoting your band, demo, CD, digital downloads, gigs or whatever it is you currently do with a guitar, instead. The gear you have is fine; you sound good.

Now, why would you do this? Because investing money in promotion will get you showing up on the radar of all those guitar, effects and amp companies that like to give you free stuff to try out because now they see you as an 'influencer'. Gladly accept any gear that's sent to you, share a photo of yourself with it on social media (might be a requirement, but do it anyway), and expect more free gear to arrive.

Tom Morello recently said that gear doesn't matter, it's just a tool to channel your creativity. Tom can say this because he still uses the same $200 rig he's been using for the last 28 years. My first guitar teacher was the same. He became a great session player, toured America, played on loads of people's stuff, yet he still used the first guitar he ever got. I can't even remember what make it was, but it was cheap-looking and ugly as hell.

At the end of the day, I'd have to agree with Tom.

14. Buy Tons of Picks

There's an incredible variety of guitar picks out there, yet most guitarists use either Jazz IIs or Jazz IIIs. Every time you're in a guitar shop buy some more. I'm a Jazz III man, but I'm still searching for that perfect pick and besides, picks are about the cheapest thing you can buy for a guitar so you can always afford to buy a ton of them. Plus, they'll replace the ones you already lost down the pick vortex.

Now is a good time to experiment with different picks because as an advancing guitarist, you have your technique to a point where it's pretty much settled as far as holding a pick, and picking techniques go. What you're looking for is the perfect pick to complement those much honed techniques, and the only way you're going to find it is to test them all out.

15. The 'Hendrix' Chord and When to Use It

The 'Hendrix' chord is the 7#9 chord found in songs such as Purple Haze, Voodoo Child, and Foxy Lady, among others. Hendrix didn't invent the chord of course, he just brought it in to push the blues envelope at the time. You probably know this chord from the above tracks, but do you know how to incorporate it into your own stuff? Here are a few ideas:

1. The 7#9 can be used as a substitute for the V chord in a blues. For example, the V chord in a blues in A would be E7, which you could replace with E7#9 to great effect.

2. It makes for an excellent tonic chord in a lot of disco/funk music from the 70s and 80s. Check out stuff like, 'Boogie Nights'.

3. It's a great tension-creator before resolving back to the I chord, be it minor, major or dominant.

4. You can play the Altered Scale over it (7th mode of the melodic minor) as it is diatonic to that scale. Here's the chord in the context of the melodic minor scale. We have a few positions for B7#9 from the C Melodic Minor scale.

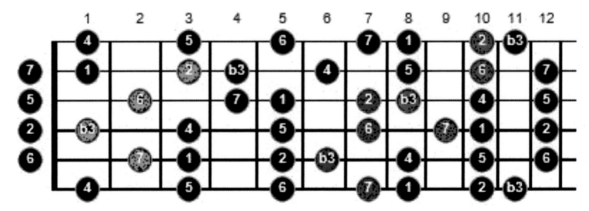

To find the corresponding scale simply play the notes from 7 to 7 using a fingering that's comfortable for you, or use the following one:

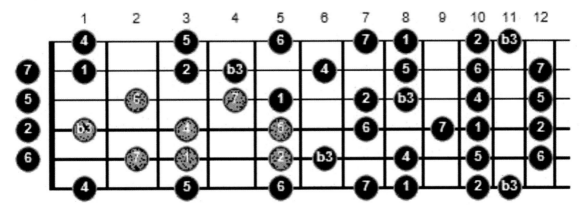

16. How to 'Johnny B. Goode' Any Scale

Unless you've been living in a cave, you've probably heard Johnny B. Goode at some point. Most of Chuck Berry's riffs in this song are made up of double-stops or diads (two notes), which is great because they're kind of in-between single notes and triads. This is also great because you can use them in solos and get away with using them as rhythm fills. Simply play the scale with its adjacent note on the string below or above and you have a diad. Here's an example with A minor pentatonic:

Now, you can do this with any scale you like and come up with some interesting results. The great thing here is that you don't have to think in terms of shapes to pull out a diad; you can probably do it without too much thinking as well, and they'll liven up your solos and rhythm playing no end.

17. Scale Fragments: Practice This to Increase Your Speed

You may have noticed that when you tune the guitar the distance between all the strings, except the G string to the B string is a perfect fourth. From the G string to the B string it's a major third which kind of offsets any pattern or shape, and requires a slightly different hand movement or fingering to accommodate it. It will really help your speed to zone in on this area of the fretboard, and just practice crossing from the G string to the B string and vice versa. Let me show you what I mean:

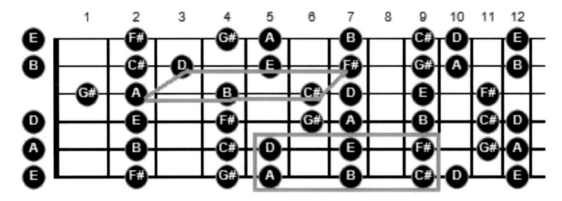

Compare the fingerings for the sets of notes on the low E and A strings with the ones on the G and B strings. They're the same set of notes, but on the G and B strings you have to alter your hand movement; this is the pattern you should zero in on and practice if you want to improve your fluidity in this part of the fretboard. Continue up the neck; there's a pattern starting on each note of the scale. This is purely mechanical and sheer repetition will solve this problem, so you could even do it while you're watching TV.

18. Repetition Is Only Half the Story

It's well-known that an absurd amount of repetition is one of the keys to monster technique, but repetition is only half the story. This is where you have to start really observing yourself and monitoring the **quality of the repetition**.

Take the six-note grouping from the last hack and play it over and over. Observe your left and right hands while standing in front of a mirror, and make sure each repetition is identical to the last. Keep going as you make the necessary adjustments, paying attention to things like economy of movement, pick control, the motion of your fretting hand, as well as any other movements involved in the execution. Focus on one hand and then the other. You should find this has a fairly instant effect on the accuracy of your playing, and is well-worth incorporating into your practice routine.

Be sure to use small fragments of any technique for this exercise in order to maximize your quality control.

19. Split the Fretboard

This is a great exercise to do if you feel you're not getting anything from scales, or you're just playing through the same old licks and runs.

Choose a familiar scale and split the fretboard as follows. We'll use the good old blues scale in G.

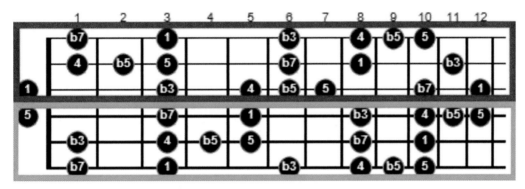

You're only allowed to play in either the blue or red area of the fretboard at any one time. This forces you to think differently and therefore come up with different ideas and runs as the same old licks are no longer available. Try it with any scale that's become a bit stale.

20. Zone in to Improve Your Phrasing

Another way to come up with new stuff or reinvent your phrasing is to zone in on one particular area of the fretboard as follows. For this exercise, it's important to restrict yourself to a fairly small area of the fretboard.

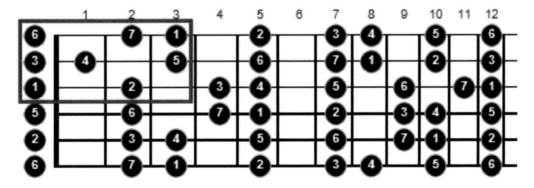

Here we have a G major scale up to the 12th fret, but in this exercise you're only allowed to use the area marked in red. You must not venture outside of this box. You can use any technique you like, as long as you stay within the box. The trick here is persistence as you'll probably run out of ideas in under 2 minutes; keep playing and I guarantee you'll become more creative and inventive with your ideas and phrasing.

21. Take Advantage of Your Own Hindsight

If you've been playing for a while, you can easily take advantage of your own hindsight. To do this simply revisit the early stages of your playing, such as:

-The songs you learned
-The music you listened to
-The books you used
-The websites you visited/videos you watched
-Basic chords, scales and arpeggios
-Any diagrams you made or things you wrote down

What you'll find is that you now see and hear these things differently, and from a different perspective. You'll notice things you didn't notice before, and these things are priceless because they're your personal insights into your own playing.

22. How to Spice Up Your Chord/Rhythm Playing

One way to come up with more interesting chords is to realize that you have a ton of options available from stuff you may already know. A C major chord appears in 3 different keys (C, F, and G), which all give you different options for extending those chords. Check out the following diagrams. I've marked a C major triad in each key which is easy to play with your first finger; it's then up to add notes into the chord that you can reach with your other three fingers. Use the diagrams below.

C Major

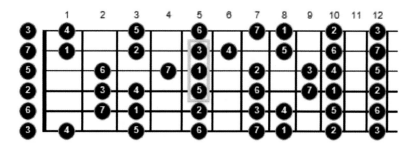

F Major

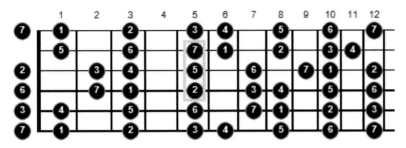

G Major

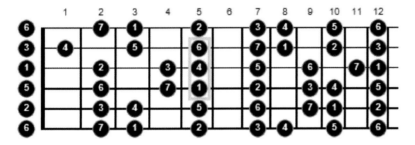

The C major triad is the same in every key, but what changes are the options you have to extend that C major triad and come up with new chords and sounds. You can even do this on the fly if you know the scale patterns well.

You can also take this idea further as C major appears in the following Melodic Minor scales.

F Melodic Minor

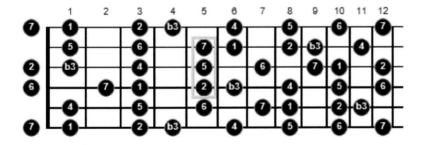

G Melodic Minor

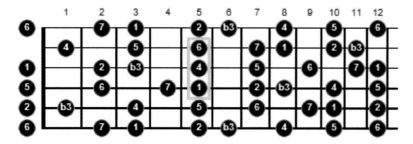

This is a great way to come up with more unusual-sounding chords, and if you think about the number of scales a C major triad appears in, the possibilities are endless.

23. How to Memorize New Material Faster

If you need to learn a bunch of new material, then slogging over it for hours on end is not the answer. If you've got five new songs to learn, you'll want to spend—at the most—20 minutes on each song, whether you finish learning it or not, then go on to the next one. I'd recommend around 15 minutes as according neuroscientists the brain cannot learn new material after 15 minutes or so. I've really found this to be true as it keeps your brain fresh, and you don't have that feeling of, 'must… get… through… this… song…' because you can come back to it fresh when its 15-minute slot comes back around. Try it with four or five songs and you'll be impressed with your progress after a couple of hours compared to spending a couple of hours on just one or two songs.

24. The Hearing Lag

Once a lot of players get to a fairly advanced level in their playing, they inevitably run into a wall with their improvisation because they start to improvise via theoretical concepts, without really hearing what they sound like. For example, you may be able to improvise using intervals like 9ths, 11ths and 13ths in your playing, perhaps through a scale pattern or an extended arpeggio shape, but away from the instrument, can you imagine/hear what this sounds like? The problem is that we don't take the time to really hear what an interval such as a #9 sounds like over a 7th chord; and this is precisely what we need to start doing. Looper pedals are great for this as you simply record the chord you want to experiment over, and 'try out' all the intervals.

I'd recommend starting with the triads from the chords below, then start adding in the 7th.

Major 7: 1, 3, 5, 7

Minor 7: 1, b3, 5, b7

Dominant 7: 1, 3, 5, b7

Half-diminished 7: 1, b3, b5, b7

These are by far the most 'in' tones over any chord, and should be explored in depth. What most books/instructors then tell you to do is to learn how all the other notes/intervals sound over these chords. I would suggest you do the same, but with special focus on **the ones you like**. As you move beyond patterns and your ear begins to catch up, you'll want to start choosing what you play over certain chords. According to your musical tastes, and the style(s) you play, you'll gravitate more to certain intervals/flavors over certain chords. This is also a great way to explore your own style on guitar, as choosing what you do and don't like helps it to emerge.

25. Beyond the 'Hendrix' Chord

Back in Hack 15 we came across the so-called 'Hendrix' chord, the 7#9. I say so-called because it was obviously being used way before Hendrix came along; even the Beatles used it. Anyway, technically the 7#9 is an **altered dominant chord**.

An altered dominant chord is basically any dominant chord with the 5th or 9th degree moved up or down a semi-tone, creating chords such as G7#5, G7b5, G7b9, and of course, G7#9. They usually come in two varieties: those that resolve to the I chord, and those that don't. The basic function of these chords is to create tension. Check out the fretboard diagram below which shows a couple of places on the neck where it's easy to grab these altered dominant chords, shown here in G. The black notes are basic dominant 7th chords and the extensions are marked as intervals below. Combine the two to create altered dominant chords. Feel free to add more than one note, such as a G7#5b9 to create even more tension!

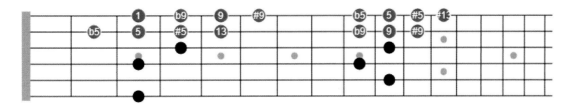

26. The Reason You Find Chord Tone Soloing Hard

As an advancing guitarist, you'll want to venture into chord tone soloing at some point. What you won't want to do is approach it the way a lot of players do, and completely miss the point.

Chord tone soloing involves purposely aiming to bring out the notes of the chord you happen to be improvising over to give your solo a melodic flavor. This kind of soloing is more pleasing to the average (non-musician) listener, who will believe that you really know what you're doing!

There are a few simple rules that you must follow at all times if you want to make chord tone soloing work in your playing:

1. **Know the chord progression, and the chord of the moment** (the chord you're playing over). Sounds obvious but a lot of guitarists are used to not really thinking about the changes and just blowing over them using one or two scales.

2. **Chord tones are not scales with fewer notes**. Hammering on the chord tones as if they were a scale with fewer notes will never do. You need to play 'on purpose', and lose the scalar-type thinking.

3. **You must know where you are and where you're going to**. It is essential to know the chord you're on and the chord you're moving to, otherwise you are simply in no man's land.

4. **Know how to find the next chord tone without thinking**. You can do this either by note name or interval, but it must be second nature.

How to Apply Chord Tones

I consider the most useful chord tones to be the 1, 3, 5, and 7 of the chord. Extended chords such as 11ths and 13ths contain other intervals, but these verge into the gray area between chord tones and the scale. A major 13th chord, for example, actually contains all the notes from the major scale; for practical purposes various tones are omitted in a maj13 chord as there's no way to play them all on guitar (unless you're into two-handed chords or have an 8 or 9 string handy).

Most lessons I've seen on chord tones take you through the whole process without considering how long the process takes, and would have you believe that you'll be soloing using chord tones within the hour. This is not the case because they seem to gloss over the most important and time-consuming step—locating and remembering where the chord tones are.

It is also not enough to just see a chord shape and head for it; for example, if the next chord is Cmaj7 and you head for a Cmaj7 chord shape you know, it won't sound convincing. What you need to be thinking is, 'C major coming up... I'm going to land on the 3rd which is E... so I need to make my way to the closest E on the fretboard'. Don't worry if this sounds a little labored, it will soon become second nature and you'll automatically land on the note you want. You can speed up this process by really getting to know the 1, 3, 5, and 7 of various chords, especially m7, 7, maj7, 9 etc. chord types.

Takeaway: Spend plenty of time getting to know where and what the chord tones are before you attempt to solo with them.

27. The Real Meaning of 'Less is More'

You've probably heard the familiar anti-shred rant about B.B. King being able to floor [insert name of shredder] with one note. This is completely subjective of course, but it teaches us a lot about less is more. What you have to consider are the more than 50 years of playing behind B.B. King's one note, which is what makes it so powerful to many. **As an advancing guitarist you should now be able to do a whole lot more with a whole lot less**. You can apply this is to virtually any area of guitar playing such as:

Soloing. You should be able to say a lot with a handful of notes, rather than running up and down scale patterns trying to find something cool, or learning yet more scales.

Technique. You shouldn't need to use every technique under the sun to get your point across anymore.

Chords. You should be able to explore and come up with endless ideas and inversions for (at least) two or three-chord progressions.

Composition. You should be able to take a simple idea and push it to its limits. Think, 'Cliffs of Dover', or 'For the Love of God'.

Appropriateness. You should be able to complement any song or piece of music you contribute to with something that fits it like a glove.

And so on... Oftentimes we think we need to do more or learn more when in actual fact, we need to do quite the opposite.

28. Stop Learning Guitar Solos

This may seem like a drastic measure but the benefits of not learning any more guitar solos (at least for while) are well-worth it. If you're in a rut with your soloing, or all your solos sound the same, or have become mindless, scalar nonsense, learning more of the same will only compound the problem. This is a great time to turn to other instruments such as the saxophone, clarinet, trumpet, violin etc. for soloing inspiration, and if you can read music or work out solos on these instruments by ear, then you have a very useful tool at your disposal. You may have heard this advice before, but it's important to know why you're doing this (or anything for that matter), as if you don't see a purpose you're unlikely to keep at it.

The purpose here is to play stuff that doesn't fall nicely on a guitar, but sounds great. The guitar can make us a little lazy in terms of playing what falls under our fingers easily, and this is a disadvantage that tends to become the cause of stale-sounding improvisations. What's more, your average saxophone player is far more melodic than your average guitarist due to the fact of having to know chords in-depth in order to produce a good solo, i.e. there's no pattern to blow up and down on a saxophone. You could start by transcribing stuff like the sax part in, 'Baker Street', by Gerry Rafferty, or the sax part in, 'Your Latest Trick', by Dire Straits. The tab for parts like these should also be easily available if you don't read music, or aren't ready to work it out by ear.

29. Sweep Picking Made Easy

As an advancing guitarist, sweep picking is probably one of those techniques you feel you should be able to do by now. I know I certainly did, and although I was never a serious shredder, I was always curious about the technique and thought it'd be useful to know. Once you reverse engineer sweep picking, you discover that the mechanics of it are far easier to digest and assimilate into your playing if you work on one hand at a time in this order:

1. **Start with you picking hand ONLY,** and just damp the strings with your fretting hand for now. The technique was named SWEEP picking for a reason, and that reason is that you must do a sweep with your picking hand, and NOT pick every note by dragging your pick across the strings. This is a sweep, almost like a quick brushstroke, so there shouldn't be any dragging of the pick to make the individual notes sound. Once this clicks and you can see the difference move on to the next step.

2. **Learn to finger-roll**. Finger-rolling is prominent in a lot of sweep arpeggios, and will lead to a lack of synchronization if you don't master it first. The technique simply involves moving the top part of your finger across two or three adjacent strings in a rolling motion so that the notes sound separately and don't bleed into each other. Practice with all four of your fretting hand fingers; yes, even your pinky.

3. **Practice each hand separately**. I can't stress this enough as each hand needs to know what it's supposed to be doing before you attempt any kind of hand-synchronization. Check out the example below and practice first with your picking hand and then with your fretting hand. When you're practicing the picking hand part, you can rest one of your fingers over the 12 fret so that the harmonics sound as you move your picking hand. This will give you more of an idea as to whether you're getting, or going to get, the right sound when you sync your hands.

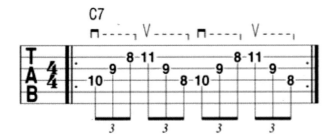

4. **Hand Synchronization**. It's time to start meshing the motions of each hand. I say meshing because you'll really need to work on sycing them together until they become one unit. Remember that your synchronizing two different motions here, so you should be speeding one hand up to compensate for the other one.

99% of the problems you may run into while learning sweep picking can be solved by going over one or all of the points above.

30. How to Play the Minor Pentatonic Scale Over Almost Anything

Who doesn't love the minor pentatonic scale? Some players love it so much that they prize it above the need to learn any other scale. It works over minor chords, and dominant chords, which just leaves major chords... You probably wouldn't think to play box 1 of the minor pentatonic over a major or even a major 7 or major 9 chords but here's how you can get away with it, and sound slick into the bargain.

Here we see a G Major scale from the nut to the 12th fret. As you may know, C Major/C Major 7 is the IV chord in the key of G Major, but check out the contents of the blue square. It's box 1 of the B Minor Pentatonic scale! Can you play B Minor Pentatonic over a C Major/Major 7 chord then? Of course you can, and it's going to sound cool because of the intervals you're (perhaps unintentionally) targeting.

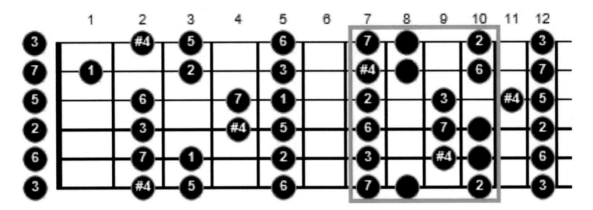

There's no root note in the scale, but you've got the 9th (2nd), the 7th, the #4 for that Lydian-esque sound, the 6th, and the major 3rd. Grab your looper pedal and try this one out over a C Major/Major 7 chord. Don't play your usual minor pentatonic licks (do try them though, because they'll sound sick) and spend some time 'getting hold of the sound'.

Check out the following diagram:

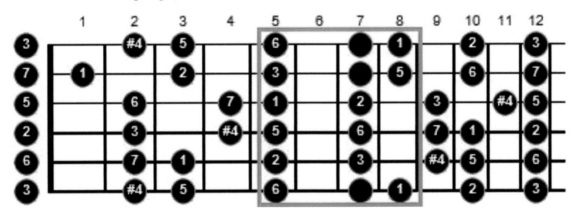

Do you see what I see? Yes, it's the most overused shape in guitar history, the A Minor Pentatonic box 1, which we can now play over C Major/Major 7. The root note C does feature here, and we've also got the major 3rd, the 6th, the 9th, and the 5th. Wait a minute, isn't this the C Major Pentatonic scale? It certainly is, this is just another way to get to it.

And finally, in case you didn't spot it.

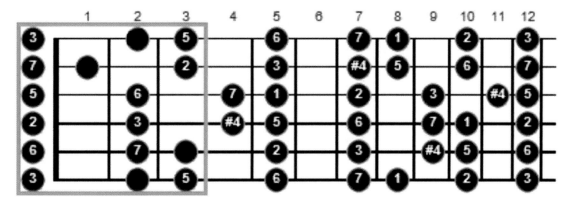

Yes, good old E Minor Pentatonic can also be played over C Major/Major 7 chords. It's going to sound a little twisted though, so make sure you spend some time getting hold of the sound. There's no root in there again, and you've got the major 3rd, 5th, 6th, 7th and 9th to play with.

Homework: Check out the key of F Major which contains C Major/C7 as its V chord, and the key of C Major to find two other minor pentatonic box 1 patterns you can play over major chords.

31. 4 Neglected Pentatonic Scales

Now that you know all the tricks and hacks for getting the most out of pentatonic scales, why not try out a few of the more underused ones?

1. The Dorian Pentatonic

If you want something that sounds more Dorian than the Dorian scale itself, then the Dorian Pentatonic Scale is for you. It's basically a minor pentatonic scale with 6 instead of the b7, and what this does is emphasize the 6, which is the interval that gives it that Dorian sound. Here's a box 1 pattern for it to start you off.

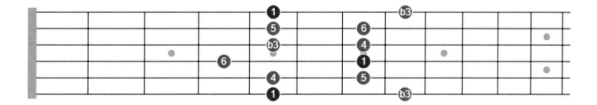

2. The Mixolydian Pentatonic

In much the same vein as the previous scale, the Mixolydian Pentatonic sounds more Mixolydian than the Mixolydian scale itself. It's basically a Mixolydian scale with the 4th and 6th removed which emphasizes the 3rd and b7. Check it out box 1.

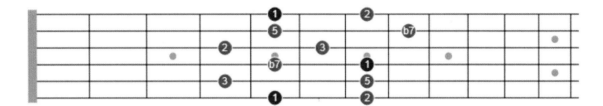

3. The Lydian Dominant Pentatonic

I love this scale because the pattern is fairly easy to remember, and it sounds sick over a dominant 7 or 9 chord or maj#11 chord. It's only one note different from the previous scale, but that #4 makes a hell of a difference.

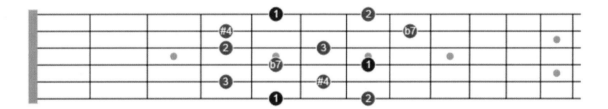

4. The Minor/Major 7 Pentatonic

If you find you're not getting anything from the melodic minor scale, try the mMaj7 pentatonic out. It's basically a melodic minor scale with the 2nd and 6th removed to really zone in on that natural 7 minor 3rd contrast. You might want to move the 7 from the B string and play it on the 4th fret of the E string if it's a bit of a stretch. Check it out.

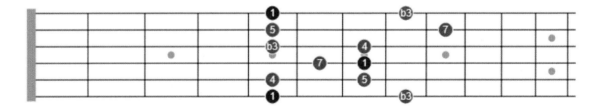

32. Are You Picking from the Right Place?

Take another look at your picking technique and check where the power or motion is actually coming from. There are three areas you can pick from:

1. **The Elbow**. This picking technique is best executed without your hand coming into contact with the guitar, and is a rotating motion which makes the pick move up and down. EVH's tremolo picking technique is a good example of this one.

2. **The Wrist**. For this picking technique the power comes from the rest, and you can rest the heel of your hand on the strings to aid damping. Guthrie Govan is a good example of a wrist-picker.

3. **The Thumb and Forefinger**. Here the power comes from the fingers you hold the pick with, and again you can rest your hand on the strings. Yngwie Malmsteen is a good example of this.

Try them all out as there may be one that works better, and faster, for you than the one you currently use. Watch your favorite players too, to see where they're picking from.

33. What Do I Use This for?

Never lose that childlike curiosity you have, especially when it comes to guitar. If you've been around children, you'll often find them asking, 'What's this for, and what's that for?' They have a burning desire to know, and their curiosity must be satisfied at all costs. The adult version of this is coming across something and not resting until you find out what it does, or how you can use it, or how you can apply it to your own life.

As an example, take an augmented chord. This is a D augmented chord.

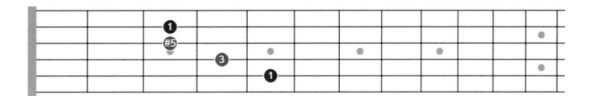

It always sounded kind of familiar to me until I realized I'd heard it used as an intro or a turnaround in a minor blues! Here it is again superimposed over a G Minor Pentatonic scale.

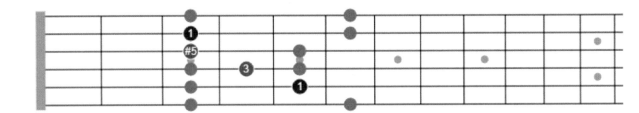

D is the V chord of G so it's a very easy way to come up with a turnaround on the fly, or an intro to a minor blues. **The point is to investigate anything you're curious about, and find a way it makes sense to you so that you can use it in your own playing.**

34. How to Know What to Learn Next

I don't think there's a set sequence of items to be learned as you progress with the guitar; I think this is more relevant in the beginning. When you reach the intermediate level it becomes a lot more difficult to know what to learn next.

Every time I reached a dead-end with my playing, or didn't know what to study next, I'd go watch a really solid guitarist; not a famous one, but just a really good guitar player who played in a local band. This is a great opportunity to put yourself in his/her shoes and ask yourself what you'd be lacking, or what you'd have to learn in order to sub for that guy or gal. If you were suddenly thrust into their shoes, what would you be able to do, and more importantly, what wouldn't you be able to do? The conclusions you reach to the latter question are the things you need to work on.

35. How to Make the Most of Backing Tracks

Backing tracks have always been around, even in the days of guitar magazines with accompanying CDs. The advent of the internet has meant that access to backing tracks of all shapes and sizes is available on a large scale, which is both good and bad depending on how you use them.

You should always have an objective in mind when you go to play over a backing track, which could be to improve your phrasing, timing, note choice, playing over changes, groove, etc., as well as some kind of diagram to refer to. The point of having the diagram there is to avoid what usually happens when you go to improvise over a backing track: you play everything you know and don't learn anything new; whereas, if you have a diagram in front of you, it forces you to think a little more and venture into other parts of the neck.

Let's say you've found a Lydian mode backing track in A. Use the diagram below which has the 'Lydian' note marked in blue and the root note marked in red to really explore the mode and see what you can come up with.

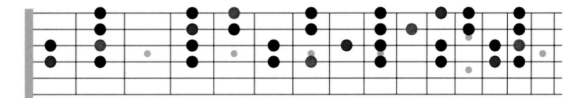

I've left out the notes on the low E and A strings because most improvisation is done on the top four strings if you think about it, and since we're in A Lydian, that low open A string is useful for bolstering the Lydian sound should you want to play chords or double-stops.

36. How to Tap into an Infinite Supply of Riffs, Licks and Ideas

I picked this hack up from Steve Vai, and it's a method he has used to come up with many of his greatest pieces of music.

What you do is simply play whatever comes into your head but record yourself while you're doing it. Once you've played through a lot of crap, or stuff you always play, the good stuff will start to come out as you'll kind of 'make space' for it. After a while you'll forget you're actually recording yourself and start to play even more interesting stuff. Once you feel you've reached your limit, stop the device you're recording with and go back over it. You might want to rest a little before you do this so that you can get some objective distance from what you're about to hear. When you listen back, look for riffs, ideas, melodies or anything that sounds like a seed that could grow into a song or be developed in some way; extract those and start working on them. You'll almost certainly find a couple of ideas in there that you never would have heard otherwise; this is the advantage of having both a subjective and objective experience of your own playing.

37. Instant Jazz/Fusion Soloing with 9-Note Scales

This was an idea I came up with for experimenting with jazz fusion improvisation to see if it was worth pursuing.

I remember asking my first guitar teacher about which scales to play over which chords, naively expecting a definitive answer, and he said, 'Well, basically you can play any note you like over any chord as long as you resolve it, and play it like you meant it'. Bearing this somewhat vague but sound advice in mind, I used it to come up with a couple of 9-note scales to experiment with jazz fusion playing.

For simplicity's sake let's say that most chords fall into one of two categories: major or minor (I didn't bother with a separate scale for 7th chords and their extensions as you can get away with playing either of the following scales over this kind of chord, plus it's jazz so don't be afraid of dissonance).

First of all, I chose 9 intervals I like playing over major chords: 1, 2, 3, 4, b5, 5, 6, b7, 7. I then mapped out the scale in a comfortable location on the fretboard.

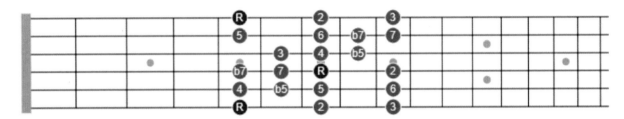

You don't have to use these intervals, you can and should choose your own. I think 9 notes in a scale is the absolute limit before venturing into shameless chromaticism.

Here's the minor version which features the following intervals: 1, 2, b3, 4, b5, 5, b6, b7, 7.

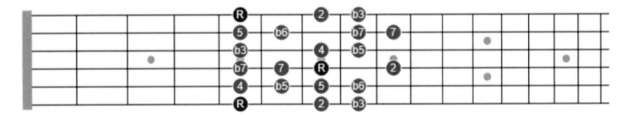

The idea here is to come up with jazz/fusion lines from the notes available. It takes a little getting used to if you haven't ventured into this style before, but you should be hearing some interesting stuff in no time. Don't worry about hitting any 'wrong notes', simply try to incorporate them into your lines.

38. How to Take the Tedium Out of Learning Arpeggios

I was never a big fan of learning arpeggios, especially through a set of shapes up and down the neck, and a lot of rote repetition. Even after I had managed to learn the clunky shapes, I never really felt comfortable using them and they always seemed forced. A few years later I came back to arpeggios but with a completely different approach.

In the diagram below you have all the notes up to the 12th fret for an **Fmaj7 arpeggio**.

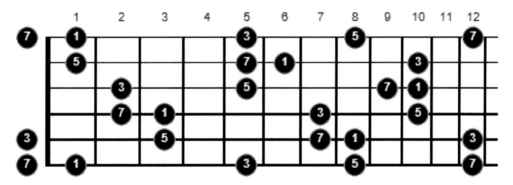

You can probably see the aforementioned tedious shapes in there, but what I want you to focus on instead is coming up with is **stuff you would actually play using the notes from an arpeggio**. If you think about it, we're just one note away from a pentatonic scale, so treat this collection of notes more like scale fragments than arpeggio patterns.

Practicing arpeggios in rigid patterns also forces you to do the most uninspiring thing you can do with an arpeggio—play the notes in order like an 'etude'. Outside of 'etude' playing, you'll want to make music with arpeggios, especially since we're dealing with the chord tones.

So, practice coming up with lines that sound good to you, and you'll soon see this reflected in your playing; subtly at first, but it will come through. If you practice arpeggios this way, what you're actually doing is practicing the fragments of the scale with the strongest notes, and this will make your overall playing sound much better.

Here are 3 more arpeggio diagrams so that you've got the most common ones covered.

F minor 7 Arpeggio

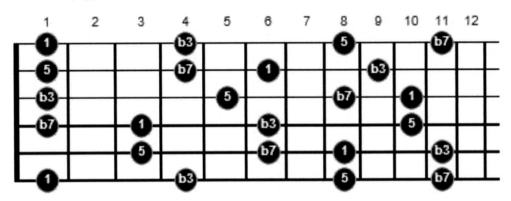

F7 Arpeggio

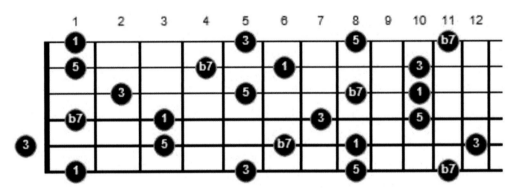

Fm7b5 Arpeggio

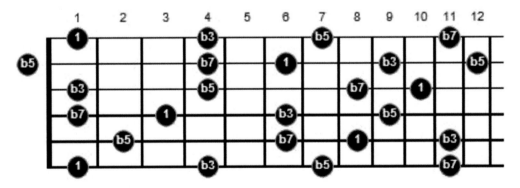

39. Improve Your Phrasing with the Pivot Technique

This is a great exercise to improve your phrasing as it forces you to do several things: 1) stay in one area of the neck, 2) resolve the phrase, and 3) use your other fingers where you normally wouldn't. There are only a couple of rules to follow.

1. Choose a scale you want to work with, and find a diagram of it like the one below, or map it out by hand. Let's say I want to improve my phrasing when I'm using the melodic minor scale.

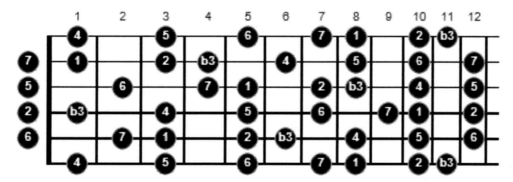

2. Plant your first finger on any of the root notes (1) on the fretboard. You are not allowed to move this finger (it must always be on or hovering above the root note), the rest of your fingers must do the work while the planted finger makes sure you resolve each phrase you come up with.

3. Now plant your second finger on the same root note, and see what you can come up with; the same rules apply.

4. Rinse and repeat for your other two fingers, and the other locations of the root note.

You should find that this exercise slows you down a little and challenges you to think in phrases rather than runs or scale patterns.

40. The Law of Overcompensation and Fretting Hand Strength

I was never a fan of doing masochistic fretting hand exercises to build up strength, especially due to their 'manufactured' nature, meaning that there was always this gap between the exercise and things you would actually play. You may have noticed that when you go back to guitar after playing bass, or even a seven or eight string guitar, the guitar is somewhat easier to play and even seems more 'controllable'. This is because you had to overcompensate your fretting hand strength to play a more physically demanding instrument. While playing bass and extended range guitars will help you build up strength in your fretting hand, you can also invoke this same 'law of overcompensation' on a regular six string by **only playing with your fretting hand**. Try it, and see what you can play. You'll find your fretting hand automatically starts to overcompensate and digs in harder; keep going until your hand starts to feel 'worked out' and then rest. When you add your picking hand back in, you should feel the difference.

41. The Best Books for Learning to Sight Read

Back at music college we had sight reading class with legendary jazz guitarist Pete Callard. If you've ever been to music college, you'll know that sight reading class (for guitarists) is about as painful as it gets, especially when your other classes are taught by Guthrie Govan, Dave Kilminster etc. Anyway, during one of those classes he became particularly frustrated and half-shouted at us, 'How can you call yourselves musicians if you can't read music?!' This rocked us to the core, and it was then that I decided to make an effort and learn to read.

You might want to consider learning to read, even if you don't think it will be useful in your line of guitar playing, because it opens up a whole new world of both material and possibilities. If you're thinking of turning pro at some point, it'll give you a huge advantage at auditions and sessions.

If you do decide to take the plunge and learn to read, **avoid guitar sight reading books at all costs**. It seems logical; you want to learn to read on guitar, so you go buy a sight reading book for guitar. Don't do it. Guitar sight reading books contain some of the dullest reading material around, and usually start with the tunes you learned on a xylophone in 3rd grade music class. I guarantee you won't get past the first 10 pages. What you should get instead are some **easy** sight reading books for other treble clef instruments such as the violin, flute, oboe, bagpipe, cor anglais, all clarinets, all saxophones, horn, trumpet, cornet, vibraphone, mandolin, etc. These kind of books contain real music, and real melodies; plus, you get to decide where to play them on the guitar neck, whereas most guitar sight reading books teach you in position.

As Steve Lukather says:

"I can't tell you how helpful knowing music theory and learning to read and write music has been. It is the language of what we do.

"You don't have to be 'Mr Sight-read', but fuck anyone who tells you it 'hurts your playing'. I have never heard such shit in my life. Knowledge is power.

"There are great players that know none of this stuff, but I bet if you asked them, 95 per cent would say they wished they did, and that they had learned it when they were young. I played by ear for the first seven years of my career, and it was very hard to go back and learn music properly, but I think it was worth it - and I use it every day.

"There is so much competition - anything that gives you the edge to get the gig and keep it seems the right way to go to me."

42. How to Find the Right Gear for You

The right gear for you is the gear that resonates with you when you pick it up or try it out. The right gear for you may not be a Fender Strat or a Gibson Les Paul, despite the incredible peer pressure there is to have these kinds of guitars. If I'm honest, I don't really like either of the above guitars, and for a long time I thought there was something wrong with me. If I pick up or have to use a Fender Strat, I'll spend most of the time trying to make it not sound like a Fender Strat, and this is a huge clue as to whether a guitar or an amp is really for you.

I'd also advise against buying a brand of guitar just because your favorite guitarist uses it, or signature models and so forth. What I would say is to check out their effects and stomp boxes as out of all the effects they could have had, they chose those ones, so there must be something worth checking out.

So, if you're going to invest in gear, invest in gear that resonates with you; not gear you think you should own. Listen to your gut feeling and shut off the voice in your head when you go to buy some gear and you won't be disappointed.

43. If You Use Tablature, You Must Do This

When I started playing around twenty-something years ago, there was still a great amount of snobbery surrounding the use of tablature instead of learning to read music. I would never discourage anyone from doing either, but if you're going to use tablature there are a couple of things you should definitely do.

The first is print it out; the second is to annotate the tab with all the dynamics you can hear in the music such as vibrato, louder notes, muting, inflections and so on. All those little nuances that most tablature doesn't have because if you don't you'll end up playing it flat without any dynamics at all. You can even create your own notation system for tablature in order to bring the music to life.

44. The Dreaded, 'Now Practice This in All 12 Keys...'

I used to get disheartened when I'd spend hours learning something in one key, and be able to pull it off only to read the phrase, 'Now practice this in all 12 keys', or something to that effect as the closing sentence in the lesson.

While it's obviously good to be able to play in all 12 keys, your practice time will be better spent truly mastering something in one key because you're creating a visualization of it on the fretboard, and the more solid that visualization becomes, the easier it will be to shift it to different keys. If you practice whatever you're learning in all 12 keys, what you'll end up with is the ability to play it in a mediocre way in all 12 keys when you could better spend your time creating a life-like representation of it in your mind which is easily transferable to other keys.

45. Is It Time to Forget Scales?

You've probably heard people saying things like, 'Yeah, you learn all that theory just to forget it and play'. What they don't tell you is that you have to make a conscious effort to do this. I remember transitioning into this by working with a couple of ideas.

The first is to improvise by moving from octave to octave over the whole fretboard with a specific tonality in mind, which could be either major, minor, dominant or something more even specific such as a mode or interval. By now you can probably see where all the octaves are, but a diagram is always useful.

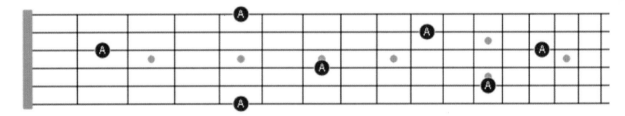

This is the kind of exercise you *can* play in all 12 keys, as I'd recommend changing root note every couple of minutes.

The other exercise involves using the scale that no one practices—the chromatic scale. Here you simply choose a chord and practice making all the notes of the chromatic scale sound good or groove over it.

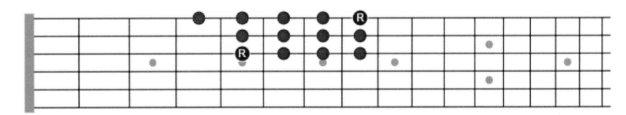

Start off with this pattern in the middle of the neck, but feel free to expand to other parts of the neck, and other keys of course.

46. More Than Repertoire

Building up a varied repertoire is critical to advancing on the guitar, but you'd be surprised at the number of players who don't really have one, or can only play bits of stuff, riffs and the odd solo. Working on a piece of music or a song should involve the following stages.

1. Start Learning the Piece

Spend around 15-20 minutes learning the piece, then do something else for a while. As we saw in Hack No.23, your brain will only absorb new material for 20 minutes at the most, so work on any new stuff in 20-minute bursts and keep coming back to it.

2. Finish Learning the Piece

A lot of players don't actually finish learning anything, and can only play bits and pieces of stuff. Stick with it until you've learned the entire piece, and there are no 'gray areas where you'll probably wing it' if you have to perform it live. At this point you shouldn't have to refer to any tablature, chord chart or notation, unless it's an incredibly long and complex piece.

3. Work it Up to Performance Level

You've finished learning the piece, and deserve a pat on the back, but there's still work to be done to get it up to performance level. Approach the piece in a relaxed way and iron out the creases as you play through it from start to finish. You'll know it's up to performance level when you can play it while thinking about what you're going to have for lunch, or you can play it all the way through several times without any clams. It's important to always finish playing the piece here, no matter how many times you screw up, as you need to feel confident that you can easily get through it, so don't stop if you make a mistake.

4. Perform It

One thing is to perform in your studio or bedroom, while another thing entirely is to play in front of people and with the unpredictable factor of a live setting. Your performance should be solid by now, but stay objective as there will still be things that can be improved upon. If you're able to record yourself, do so as you'll notice things you wouldn't notice otherwise.

47. Make Time for Noodling

Noodling, the act of undisciplined practicing and mindlessly meandering up and down the fretboard, is somewhat frowned upon in the guitar world, but is it all that bad?

I always make time to noodle because to me it's like searching for, or playing around with an idea in an almost meditative state. States such as these are indispensable for encouraging creativity, as no one ever feels under pressure when they're noodling. I would even go as far as to say that the more you noodle, the more you need to relax; in this sense it's somewhat akin to doodling.

Musicians are often drawn to things, or substances, that make them relax because to do your best playing you have to be completely at ease with yourself. So, instead of consuming vast quantities of stimulants, dedicate a little time each day to noodling, or what I like to call, 'guided noodling'. This is where you noodle yourself into a meditative state until you find something you like, then gradually reduce the options around it until you come up with a riff, or a melody of some sort. There's a great video on YouTube of Dave Matthews talking about his guitar style where he begins to noodle on a repeating phrase and soon starts to put words to it; this is the state you're aiming for.

Who said noodling was unproductive?

48. A Healthy Obsession You Should Have

You don't need me to tell you that access to information has changed the world around us immensely in the last 20 years; but, it's a double-edged sword as we have the answers to everything at our fingertips, yet lack the discipline to stay focused on one thing for any length of time. We're always ready to jump ship to the next video, the next app, the next method, etc., at the drop of a hat.

In the pre-internet world, learning guitar revolved around the few magazines that were available, finding people who were better than you to teach you, getting together with like-minded friends to work stuff out, and above all just listening to music and learning from it.

I remember a handful of tapes and CDs that I just wore out trying to learn every song off of them. The same is true of the great improvisers; the young apprentice finds one record/tape/early CD that they fall in love with. They then wear it out listening to every note and absorbing every last detail. Compare that to today's world of too much choice, and instant access to every album every released, meaning this type of healthy obsession with one recording is dying out.

For me it was Blood Sugar Sex Magic by the Red Hot Chili Peppers; I probably spent the best part of 2 years learning every single song, lick, solo and riff off of that album, most of which I can still remember 25 years later which goes to show how deep a learning experience it was. You may have had similar obsessions in your first few years of playing, and now's a great time to get obsessed again especially if you want to get (deeper) into a style like jazz, prog, or fusion.

49. How to Play Over Changes without Getting Frustrated

A critical development for the advancing guitarist is to transition from blowing over a set of changes with one scale, usually the pentatonic, to outlining the changes or 'playing the changes'. Many players tend to dive in at the deep end here and end up getting frustrated. If you're just starting to venture into playing the changes, I'd recommend not straying too far from the blues for the time being. A tune like, 'Sunshine of Your Love', is a great tune to practice playing the changes in a basic way because although it's a blues, there's plenty of room for jazz-blues style phrasing as it's not a four-on-the-floor rocker.

Look at the following three diagrams; there is one for each chord in the progression, which is a I, IV, V in D.

Over the I chord we'll play the D Minor Pentatonic scale to keep things simple:

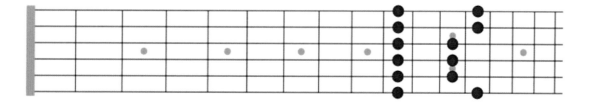

Then over the IV chord (G7), we'll stay in the same place on the neck and add in a fragment of the G Blues scale:

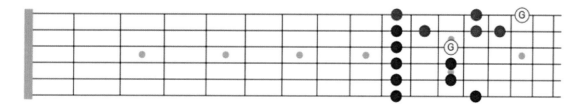

When we go to the V chord (A7), we stay in the same position again, and superimpose the A Blues scale:

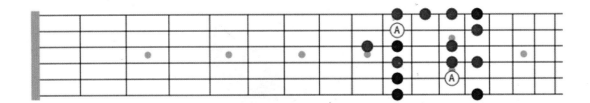

Notice how we did this in steps, and stayed in the same place on the fretboard to avoid jumping in at the deep end and getting frustrated. The blues is a great place to start for playing the changes as it combines familiar territory with a new approach.

50. Are There Any Skeletons in Your Musical Closet?

Last but not least, something that will inevitably hold you back from becoming an advanced guitarist is avoiding the difficult areas of learning to play, and never straying too far outside your comfort zone. Skills like ear training, transcribing, more complex music theory concepts, difficult techniques, sight reading and so forth should no longer be avoided as they become skeletons in your musical closet, and will invariably come back to haunt you. You probably know what you should be learning, and right now is always the best time to start learning it. We've covered an immense amount of ground in this book, and I hope to have propelled you forward into advanced territory—just make sure to clean out your closet along the way!

More from Unlock the Guitar

Visit www.unlocktheguitar.net for more insight, lessons, tutorials and books.

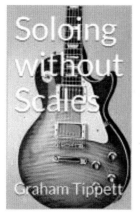  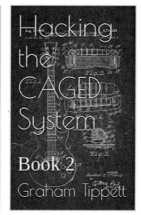 

  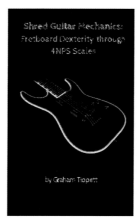 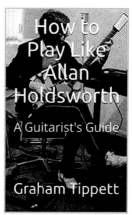